CONTENT

D0800065

Acknowledgements

We would like to thank Joy and John Pinkham for the use of their home. Louise Woodridge, Katie O'Neill, Jacks Waters (Home Economist) Katharine Ibbs (Food Stylist) for their patience and hard work. John Roan Photography in Northampton for their inspired photography. Churchs China Store in Northampton for loaning us chinaware and props. Published by Soutar Print in Northampton. Copyright©LesleyWaters 2003.

meditterranean platter

SERVES 6-8

for the marinated olives

1 x 340g jar stuffed green or pitted black olives, drained
2 tbsp extra virgin olive oil
few sprigs of fresh thyme
2 tsp coriander seeds, crushed

for the sesame houmous

220g ready-made houmous
1 tbsp extra virgin olive oil
2 tbsp sesame seeds, toasted

for the bruschetta

1 small baguette, cut into 8 slices
1 tbsp olive oil
1 x 250g Camembert
1 roasted red pepper from a jar, drained, and thinly sliced
small bunch of basil, leaves roughly torn

to serve

225g cherry tomatoes on the vine
4 pitta breads, warmed and cut into strips

1. Preheat the oven to 200C/400F/Gas Mark 6.

2. Toss the olives with the olive oil, thyme and coriander. Place in a serving bowl and set aside.

3. Spoon the houmous into a serving bowl, drizzle over the oil and scatter over the sesame seeds. Set to one side.

4. Arrange the baguette slices on a baking sheet and drizzle over the oil. Bake in the oven for 8-10 minutes until golden and crisp. Set aside to cool.

5. Slice the Camembert into wedges, place on the bruschetta, and grind over a little black pepper. Top with slices of red pepper and the basil leaves.

luxury prawn cocktail

SERVES 4

4 tbsp mayonnaise
4 tbsp Greek yoghurt
2 tbsp lime pickle
2 little gem lettuces, washed
32 tiger prawns, cooked and peeled
juice of 1 lime
freshly ground black pepper

1. In a small bowl mix together the mayonnaise, yoghurt and lime pickle.

2. Arrange the little gem leaves on four serving plates and top each with eight prawns.

3. Spoon the sauce over the prawns, squeeze over a little lime juice and grind over a little black pepper.

4. Serve with brown bread and butter or warm chapatti bread.

brie with plum compote

SERVES 8-10

for the plum compote

900g plums, halved and stoned
25g butter
115g soft brown sugar
1 tsp ground cinnamon
juice and finely grated zest of 1 orange

1 x 900g Brie cheese
freshly ground black pepper

1. Preheat the oven to 200C/400F/Gas Mark 6.

2. Place the plum compote ingredients in a pan and bring to the boil, stirring gently.

3. Cover and simmer for 5 minutes, then remove the lid and simmer for a further 8-10 minutes or until the plums are just soft.

4. Place the Brie in a shallow ovenproof serving dish. Season well with black pepper and spoon the plum compote over it.

5. Place in the oven for 8-10 minutes or until the Brie is warm and softening. Serve straightaway with blue poppy seed bread (see page 18).

cracked pepper and date bread

SERVES 8

675g strong white flour, plus extra for kneading
2 tsp mixed peppercorns, crushed
2 tsp salt
1 1/2 tsp quick yeast
2 tbsp olive oil
350g soft and juicy dates, roughly chopped

1. In a large bowl, stir together the flour, peppercorns, salt and yeast. Stir in the olive oil and approximately 425ml warm water to form a soft dough. Turn out on to a lightly floured surface and knead for 10 minutes until smooth and elastic.

2. Place the dough in a large, lightly oiled bowl. Cover and leave in a warm place for about an hour or until doubled in size.

3. Preheat the oven to 200F/400F/Gas Mark 6.

4. Knead the dough on a lightly floured surface and incorporate the dates. Shape the dough into two rounds and place on a lightly floured baking tray. Using a sharp knife, slash the top of the loaves.

5. Bake for 40-45 minutes, then allow to cool on a wire rack. Serve with chillied feta or good strong Cheddar cheese.

chillied feta

SERVES 4

225g feta cheese, cut into slices
2 hot red chilli peppers from a jar, drained, de-seeded and finely chopped

Ingredients listed in green are available from Julian Graves

1 hot green chilli from a jar, drained, de-seeded and finely chopped
1 tbsp extra virgin olive oil
handful of small mint sprigs, chopped
freshly ground black pepper

1. Place the feta on a serving plate and sprinkle over the chillies.

2. Drizzle over the olive oil and scatter over the mint. Lightly season with black pepper.

3. Leave to marinate for 30 minutes at room temperature. Serve with cracked pepper and date bread.

nutty baked camembert

SERVES 4

2 x 250g boxed Camembert cheeses
4 tbsp white wine
75g shelled walnuts
few sprigs of thyme
freshly ground black pepper

1. Preheat the oven to 190C/375F/Gas Mark 5. Unwrap the Camemberts and return them to their boxes, removing any plastic labels. Place the boxes onto a baking tray. Tie round with string to secure the boxes (do not use plastic-coated string!).

2. Pierce the rind of the cheeses with a skewer and sprinkle over the wine. Make a few slashes into the Camembert and stud with the walnuts and thyme. Grind over a little black pepper.

3. Bake for 10-12 minutes or until the Camembert is just runny.

4. Serve the Camembert with oatcakes and dip away.

Ingredients listed in green are available from Julian Graves

corn **bread** and guacamole

SERVES 6

280g cornmeal or fine semolina
85g plain flour
2 tsp bicarbonate of soda
salt and freshly ground black pepper
1 egg
150ml milk
425ml buttermilk or natural yoghurt
1 x 400g can sweetcorn, drained
3 hot green chillies from a jar, drained, de-seeded and chopped
3 hot red chillies from a jar, drained, de-seeded and chopped
4 tbsp chopped fresh parsley

for the guacamole

2 medium ripe avocado pears, stoned and peeled
1 small onion, grated
lime juice to taste
1 tbsp tomato chutney
1 tbsp olive oil
1 ripe tomato, finely chopped
1 clove garlic, crushed
1-2 hot chilli peppers from a jar, drained, de-seeded and finely chopped

1. Preheat the oven to 200C/400F/Gas Mark 6. Line an approximately 25cm shallow tin or small roasting tin with baking parchment.

2. In a large bowl combine the cornmeal, flour and bicarbonate of soda, and season well. In a jug combine the egg, milk and buttermilk.

3. Pour the contents of the jug into the bowl of dry ingredients and lightly combine (do not over-stir, over-mixing will cause the cornbread to be tough). Stir in the corn, chillies and parsley.

4. Pour the batter into the prepared tin and bake for 25-30 minutes until firm and golden on top.

5. Meanwhile, make the guacamole. In a bowl, mash the avocados and stir in the remaining ingredients. Season to taste.

6. To serve, cut the cornbread into chunks and serve warm with the guacamole.

warm chorizo salad

SERVES 4

2 tbsp olive oil
225g chorizo sausage, sliced
225g beef tomatoes, roughly chopped
3 tbsp balsamic vinegar
pinch of dried oregano
2 baby gem lettuces, washed and shredded

1. In a non-stick frying pan, heat the oil. Add the chorizo and fry for 1-2 minutes until lightly browned.

2. Add the tomatoes, vinegar and oregano and simmer for 2-3 minutes until the tomatoes are just softened but holding their shape.

3. Arrange the crisp shredded leaves on a large serving platter, and spoon over the hot chorizo and tomatoes. Drizzle with the pan juices and serve at once with crusty bread.

blue poppy seed bread

SERVES 8

675g strong white bread flour, plus extra for kneading
2 tsp salt
1 tsp freshly ground black pepper
1 1/2 tsp quick yeast
2 tbsp olive oil
2 tbsp blue poppy seeds
115g unsalted butter, softened

1. In a large bowl, sift together the flour and salt. Stir in the pepper and yeast.

2. Stir in the olive oil and approximately 425ml warm water to form a soft dough.

3. Turn the dough out on to a lightly floured surface and knead for 10 minutes until smooth and elastic. Place the dough in a large, lightly oiled bowl. Cover and leave in a warm place until doubled in size.

4. Preheat the oven to 220C/425F/Gas Mark 7.

5. Beat the poppy seeds and butter together, and set to one side.

6. Turn out the dough and knead again for 2 minutes. Using a little flour, roll the dough out into a large rectangle of about 40 x 30cm. Spread the poppy-seed butter over the surface of the dough. Roll up from the long end into a sausage shape. Place on a baking tray, seam side down, and leave to prove for 10 minutes.

7. Bake for 25-30 minutes until risen and golden. Cool on a wire rack.

chicken satay

SERVES 4

2 large skinless, boneless chicken breasts
1 tbsp groundnut oil

for the marinade

1 small onion, finely chopped
1 clove garlic, crushed
1 tbsp grated fresh root ginger
1 tbsp light muscovado sugar
1 tsp each of ground coriander and ground turmeric
1/2 tsp each of chilli powder and ground cumin
100ml coconut milk

for the peanut sauce

4 tbsp crunchy peanut butter
100ml coconut milk
1 tbsp soy sauce
1 tsp brown sugar
1 hot red chilli pepper from a jar, drained, de-seeded and finely chopped

1. Soak approximately 20 bamboo skewers in cold water for 2 hours.

2. Place all the marinade ingredients in a food processor and whiz until smooth. Pour into a bowl.

3. Cut the chicken into thin strips (approximately 5cm long and 2cm wide) and put in the bowl with the marinade. Cover and chill for 2 hours.

4. Put all the ingredients for the peanut sauce into a small saucepan with 3 tbsp water. Stir over a medium heat for 2-3 minutes until smooth. Keep warm.

5. Take the skewers out of the water and thread the chicken pieces on to them, making sure the sharp ends are covered with a little bit of chicken.

6. Heat a large frying pan with the oil and fry the chicken for 4-5 minutes until cooked through.

7. Serve with the warm peanut sauce.

indian platter

SERVES 4

for the apple, red onion and tomato relish

2 dessert apples, halved, cored and chopped
5 tomatoes, chopped
55g raisins, chopped
1 tbsp extra virgin olive oil
juice of 1 lemon
salt and freshly ground black pepper

1 x 200g packet black pepper pappadums
250g roast spiced nuts
1 x 190g jar Tien carrot and tamarind
1 x 190g jar mango chutney

for the raita

200ml natural yoghurt
2 tbsp chopped fresh mint

1. Combine all the ingredients for the relish together and season well. Cover and allow to stand for 30 minutes. Spoon into a serving dish.

2. Cook the pappadums according to packet instructions, and set to one side.

3. Place the spiced nuts in a serving dish. Spoon the tien of carrot and tamarind and the mango chutney into serving bowls.

4. Mix the raita ingredients together and season with black pepper. Spoon into a serving bowl.

5. Arrange everything on a platter and allow guests to help themselves.

Ingredients listed in green are available from Julian Graves

mediterranean stuffed
chicken with lemon
pasta

SERVES 4

4 small boneless, skinless chicken breasts
2 tbsp olive oil
juice and finely grated zest of 1 lemon
salt and freshly ground black pepper
16 black olives, pitted and finely chopped
4 sun-dried tomatoes, soaked as per packet instructions and finely chopped
2 tbsp chopped fresh flat-leaf parsley
4 slices Parma ham
350g dried spaghetti
200ml double cream
2 tbsp basil leaves, torn

1. Place the chicken in a shallow dish, and drizzle over the olive oil and half of the lemon juice. Season well with black pepper. Leave to marinate for at least 20 minutes. Set the remaining lemon juice and zest to one side for the pasta sauce.

2. In a small bowl, mix together the olives, tomatoes and parsley. Season well.

3. Using a sharp knife cut the chicken breasts almost in half horizontally and open out. Spoon the olive mixture on to one half of the breast and fold over the remaining half to enclose the stuffing. Wrap each breast with a slice of Parma ham around the centre.

4. Cook the spaghetti in plenty of boiling water according to packet instructions.

5. Heat a griddle pan, and sear the chicken for 2 minutes each side. Cover the pan loosely with foil, turn down the heat and cook for a further 8-10 minutes or until cooked through. Remove from the heat and allow to rest

whilst making the sauce for the pasta.

6. In a small saucepan heat the cream with the lemon zest and season well. Bring to the boil and simmer for 2-3 minutes. Stir in the reserved lemon juice.

7. Drain the pasta and toss with the sauce and half of the basil. Divide between four serving bowls.

8. Slice each chicken breast in half on the diagonal and place on top of the pasta. Scatter over the remaining basil and finish with an extra grinding of black pepper. Serve straightaway.

grilled lamb steaks with shallot and olive compote

SERVES 4

3 tbsp olive oil
juice of 1/2 lemon
1 clove garlic, crushed
2 sprigs thyme
4 x 150g lamb leg steaks

for the compote

2 tbsp olive oil
6 shallots, halved
pinch of sugar
2 cloves garlic, crushed
150ml red wine
150ml port
12 pitted green olives
12 pitted black olives
175g raisins
1 bay leaf
1 sprig thyme

1. In a shallow dish, mix together the olive oil, lemon juice, garlic and thyme. Lay in the lamb steaks and toss well in the marinade. Leave to marinate for 2 hours or longer if possible.

2. For the compote, heat the olive oil in a shallow pan. Add the shallots and sugar and cook over a medium heat for 5 minutes until golden all over. Stir in the garlic, red wine, port, olives, raisins, bay and thyme. Cover and simmer for 20 minutes.

3. Heat a griddle pan until hot. Remove the lamb steaks from the marinade and cook for 5-7 minutes each side, depending on how you like them cooked.

4. Serve each steak with the shallot and olive compote and roasted new potatoes.

Ingredients listed in green are available from Julian Graves

luxury lasagne

SERVES 6

450g good-quality lean beef mince
1 x 350g jar tomato and basil sauce
200ml red wine
salt and freshly ground black pepper
300ml double cream
115g extra mature Cheddar, grated
1 large egg, beaten
freshly grated nutmeg
450g baby button mushrooms, cleaned
2 cloves garlic, crushed
12 sheets fresh lasagne

1. Preheat the oven to 180C/350F/Gas Mark 4.

2. Heat a large non-stick saucepan until hot. Add the mince and fry for 4-5 minutes until browned. Add the tomato and basil sauce and the wine, season to taste, and simmer for 20-25 minutes.

3. Meanwhile in a large bowl stir together the cream, grated cheese and egg, and season with a good grating of nutmeg and black pepper.

4. Place the mushrooms in a bowl, add 6 tbsp of the cheese sauce and the crushed garlic, and gently combine.

5. Take a small non-stick roasting tin (about 20 x 6cm) or a shallow ovenproof dish, and spoon in half the meat sauce. Scatter over half the coated mushrooms and top with six sheets of lasagne. Top with the remaining meat sauce, the remaining mushrooms and the remaining lasagne sheets.

6. Pour over the remaining cheese sauce and bake in the oven for about 25 minutes until bubbling and golden.

beef and lentil
rogan josh

SERVES 4

150g red split lentils
2 tbsp sunflower oil
450g lean braising steak, cut into 2.5cm chunks
2 onions, sliced
2 tbsp rogan josh paste
1 x 400g can chopped tomatoes
1.2 litres vegetable stock
150g baby spinach leaves
salt and freshly ground black pepper

to serve

natural yoghurt
naan breads

1. Place the lentils in a pan of cold water, boil for 10 minutes, then drain and set to one side.

2. Heat the oil in a large pan. Add the braising steak and cook for 2 minutes, browning all over. Remove from the pan and set aside.

3. Add the onions to the pan and cook for 8 minutes until softened.

4. Return the beef to the pan. Stir in the rogan josh paste, tomatoes, stock and lentils. Bring to the boil then simmer gently for 1 1/2 hours.

5. Stir in the spinach, which will immediately wilt, and season to taste. Serve with a dollop of natural yoghurt and warm naan bread.

lemon and sesame chicken

SERVES 4

450g boneless, skinless chicken breasts, cut into chunks
3 tbsp lemon juice
2 tbsp olive oil
2 tbsp dark soy sauce
2 cloves garlic, crushed
2 tbsp runny honey
3 tbsp sesame seeds, toasted

to serve

150g ready-made houmous
4 tbsp Greek yoghurt
mini pitta breads
crisp lettuce leaves, shredded
1/2 cucumber, shredded
2 carrots, grated

1. In a bowl, toss the chicken with the lemon juice, olive oil, soy sauce, garlic and honey. Set to one side for 20 minutes.

2. Preheat the oven to 200C/400F/Gas Mark 6.

3. Transfer the chicken with its marinade to a shallow roasting tin and cook for 15-20 minutes until cooked through.

4. Remove the chicken from the oven and sprinkle over the sesame seeds.

5. Mix together the houmous and Greek yoghurt. Set to one side.

6. To serve, heat and split the pittas. Fill with lettuce, cucumber and grated carrot and top with the lemon and sesame chicken. Finish with a drizzle of houmous sauce.

morrocan lamb
flatbread

SERVES 8

225g pizza dough mix
4 tbsp sun-dried tomato paste
300g lean minced lamb
1 Moroccan harissa spice mill
1 clove garlic, crushed
1 large red onion, finely chopped
85g dried apricots, finely diced
85g Lexia raisins
3 tbsp pine nuts, toasted
2 tbsp chopped flat-leaf parsley

for the cheese sauce

25g butter
25g plain flour
300ml milk
55g mature Cheddar, grated
pinch of freshly grated nutmeg
freshly ground black pepper

1. Preheat the oven to 200C/400F/Gas Mark 6.

2. To make the cheese sauce, melt the butter in a small pan, stir in the flour and cook for 1 minute. Gradually add the milk, whisking all the time. Cook over a gentle heat for 5 minutes. Stir in the Cheddar and season with nutmeg and black pepper. Set aside

3. Make up the pizza dough as directed on the packet and use to line a shallow baking tray.

4. To assemble, spread the dough evenly with the tomato paste. Top with the minced lamb. Grind over with the harissa spice mill (approx. 2 tsp).

Ingredients listed in green are available from Julian Graves

5. Mix the garlic with the onion and sprinkle over the lamb. Top with the apricots and raisins.

6. Spoon over the cheese sauce and bake for about 20-25 minutes until cooked and golden.

7. Scatter over the pine nuts and parsley and serve straightaway.

chickpea spiced
cumin puffs

MAKES 4

1 tbsp sunflower oil
1 onion, chopped
1 tbsp ground cumin
225g baby leaf spinach
1 x 410g can chickpeas, drained and rinsed
salt and freshly ground black pepper
375g ready-rolled puff pastry
1 egg, beaten
1 tbsp cumin seeds

1. Preheat the oven to 200C/400F/Gas Mark 6.

2. In a large pan, heat the oil. Add the onion and cook for 5-6 minutes until soft and golden.

3. Add the ground cumin and the spinach and cook for 1 minute until the spinach wilts. Remove from the heat and stir in the chickpeas. Season to taste and set aside to cool.

4. Roll out the pastry into a large square approximately 1cm thick. Cut out four rounds about 18cm in diameter.

5. Divide the spinach and chickpea mixture between the circles, leaving a border around the edge. Brush each border with beaten egg and fold over to seal the edges together.

6. Transfer the pasties to a baking tray. Brush each with a little more egg and scatter over the cumin seeds. Bake for 12-15 minutes until puffed and golden.

Ingredients listed in green are available from Julian Graves

aubergine stack with soured cream and salsa

SERVES 4

4 medium aubergines, cut into approx. 2.5cm slices
4 tbsp olive oil
salt and freshly ground black pepper
4 tbsp soured cream
1 tbsp each of chopped fresh mint and basil

for the tomato salsa

1 roasted red pepper from a jar, drained and finely diced
4 ripe tomatoes, diced
2 spring onions, finely chopped
1 tbsp extra virgin olive oil
pinch of caster sugar
1 clove garlic, crushed
Zulu chilli sauce to taste

1. Preheat the oven to 220C/425F/Gas Mark 7.

2. Place the aubergine slices and olive oil in an ovenproof dish. Toss together and season well. Bake the aubergine in the oven for 20-25 minutes, until just softened and golden. Set to one side to cool.

3. Meanwhile make the tomato salsa, in a bowl, combine the red pepper, tomatoes, spring onions, olive oil, sugar, garlic and a dash of Zulu chilli sauce to get the heat you want. Season to taste.

4. To assemble the stack, place a layer of aubergine slices, overlapping, on the base of a large serving dish. Spoon over some of the tomato salsa and a little soured cream. Continue to layer upwards in this way with all the aubergines and tomato salsa. Finish with a final layer of tomato salsa and soured cream. Scatter over the mint and basil.

Ingredients listed in green are available from Julian Graves

red lentil and pesto pie

SERVES 4

450g ready-made shortcrust pastry
5 tbsp ready-made fresh pesto
175g red lentils, cooked, drained and cooled
freshly ground black pepper
7 medium eggs
4 spring onions, finely chopped
50g Parmesan, freshly grated

1. Preheat the oven to 200C/400F/Gas Mark 6.

2. On a lightly floured surface, roll out two-thirds of the pastry until large enough to line a 23cm flan tin. Fit the pastry into the tin but do not trim the edges.

3. In a large bowl, toss together the pesto and lentils. Season with black pepper and spoon into the pastry case.

4. Crack six of the eggs straight into the pie over the lentils, taking care not to break the yolks. Scatter over the spring onions and Parmesan, and grind over a little black pepper.

5. Beat the remaining egg, for the glaze.

6. On a lightly floured surface, roll out the remaining pastry until large enough to form a lid. Brush the edges of the pie with the beaten egg and lay over the lid. Gently push the edges to seal with the base, trimming off any excess pastry.

7. Crimp the pie edges and brush the lid with the beaten egg to glaze.

8. Bake in the oven for 35-40 minutes until golden.

roasted vegetable couscous with tahini cream

SERVES 4

1 red pepper, de-seeded
1 yellow pepper, de-seeded
1 large aubergine
2 medium courgettes
1 large red onion, cut into wedges
5 tbsp olive oil
salt and freshly ground black pepper
250g cherry tomatoes
250g couscous
juice of 1/2 lemon

for the tahini cream

3 tbsp tahini paste
juice of 1 small orange
90ml Greek yoghurt
1 tsp ground cumin
paprika for dusting
2 tbsp roughly chopped fresh flat-leaf parsley

1. Preheat the oven to 220C/425F/Gas Mark 7.

2. Prepare the peppers, aubergine and courgettes by cutting them into approximately 4cm chunks. Place in a roasting tin and toss with the onion wedges and 3 tbsp of the olive oil. Season well.

3. Roast the vegetables in the oven for 20 minutes, then add the cherry tomatoes and roast for a further 15 minutes until cooked and lightly charred.

4. Place the couscous in a large bowl and pour over 300ml boiling water. Set

aside for 5 minutes. Fluff the couscous up with a fork and stir in the remaining olive oil and the lemon juice. Season well.

5. To make the tahini cream, in a small bowl combine the tahini paste with the orange juice. Add the yoghurt and cumin and season to taste. Set to one side.

6. To serve, spread the couscous out on a large serving dish. Pile the roasted vegetables on top of the couscous. Serve the tahini cream on the side in a separate serving bowl, sprinkled with a little paprika and parsley. This dish is delicious warm or cold.

trio cheese
pepper pasta

SERVES 4-6

1 x 465g jar roasted peppers, drained and roughly chopped
150g ricotta cheese
150g mascarpone cheese
100g Parmesan, freshly grated
salt and freshly ground black pepper
28 large dried pasta shells
200ml crème fraîche
100ml milk
1 tbsp basil leaves, torn

1. Place the peppers, ricotta, mascarpone and half the Parmesan into a food processor, and process until smooth. Season well.

2. Cook the pasta shells according to packet instructions. Drain well.

3. Preheat the oven to 200C/400F/Gas Mark 6.

4. Fill the shells with the red pepper and cheese mixture and place in a single layer in a large, shallow ovenproof dish.

5. Beat together the crème fraîche, milk and remaining Parmesan, and season well. Pour over the pasta shells.

6. Bake for 15-20 minutes until golden and bubbling hot. Scatter over the basil and serve with a lightly dressed baby leaf salad.

roast salmon with
peppercorn sauce

SERVES 4

750g Charlotte potatoes, halved
2 bay leaves
4 tbsp olive oil
4 x 150g skinless, boneless thick salmon fillets
juice of 1 lemon
salt and freshly ground black pepper
2 roasted red peppers from a jar, drained and sliced

for the peppercorn sauce

150ml white wine vinegar
juice of 1 large orange
2 tbsp mixed peppercorns, crushed
1 shallot, finely chopped
150ml double cream

1. Preheat the oven to 190C/375F/Gas Mark 5.

2. Place the potatoes and bay leaves in a roasting tin and toss with 3 tbsp of the olive oil. Roast for 45 minutes.

3. Place the salmon in a shallow dish and drizzle over the remaining oil and the lemon juice. Season well.

4. Arrange the salmon fillets and sliced peppers on top of the potatoes in the tin, and cook for a further 8-10 minutes.

5. Meanwhile, make the sauce. Place the vinegar, orange juice, peppercorns and shallot in a shallow pan and boil for 1-2 minutes. Add the cream, bring to the boil and simmer for 30 seconds. Season to taste.

6. Serve the roast salmon, potatoes and peppers with the peppercorn sauce. Serve with green beans, mange tout or sugar-snap peas.

Ingredients listed in green are available from Julian Graves

crab and mango tart with chilli dressing

SERVES 8

350g ready-made shortcrust pastry
4 tbsp mango chutney
3 tbsp chopped fresh coriander
350g white crabmeat, fresh or frozen defrosted
2 eggs
2 egg yolks
325ml crème fraîche
salt and freshly ground black pepper

for the dressing

4 spring onions, finely chopped
juice of 1 lime
2 hot red chilli peppers from a jar, drained, de-seeded and finely chopped
3 tbsp soy sauce
6 tbsp sunflower oil
1 tsp caster sugar

1. Preheat the oven to 190C/375F/Gas Mark 5.

2. On a lightly floured surface, roll out the pastry and use to line a 25cm loose-bottomed tart tin. Cover and place in the fridge for 15 minutes.

3. Line the pastry tart case with greaseproof paper and fill with baking beans. Bake in the oven for 10-15 minutes. Remove the greaseproof paper and beans and return the tart case to the oven for a further 3-5 minutes until it is just cooked. Reduce the heat to 180C/375F/Gas Mark 4.

4. In a small bowl, mix together the mango chutney and coriander and spread over the base of the tart case. Scatter over the crabmeat.

5. In a bowl combine the eggs and egg yolks with the crème fraîche, and season well. Pour into the tart case.

6. Return the tart to the oven for 30-35 minutes or until just set.

7. Meanwhile, make the dressing. In a small bowl, whisk all the ingredients together with 1 tbsp water. Season to taste.

8. Serve the tart warm or cold with a drizzling of chilli dressing.

tuna em panada

SERVES 4

450g ready-made shortcrust pastry
plain flour for rolling
25g butter
1 tbsp olive oil
2 large onions, sliced
1 tsp caster sugar
4 tbsp chopped flat-leaf parsley
50g sun-dried tomatoes, soaked as per packet instructions
and cut into strips
1 x 200g can tuna in oil, drained
1 tbsp capers, rinsed and roughly chopped
2 plum tomatoes, roughly chopped
12 black olives, pitted and chopped
salt and freshly ground black pepper
1 egg yolk

1. Preheat the oven to 200C/400F/Gas Mark 6.

2. On a lightly floured surface, roll out half of the pastry into a
rectangle approximately 20 x 25cm. Transfer to a baking tray and place
in the fridge to chill for 10 minutes.

3. Prick the pastry base all over with a fork and bake for 12-15 minutes,
until golden brown. Remove from the oven and allow to cool.

4. In a frying pan, heat the butter with the olive oil. Add the sliced
onions and sprinkle with the sugar. Fry the onion over a low heat until
golden and caramelised. This may take up to 20 minutes. Set aside to
cool slightly, then stir in the parsley.

5. In a bowl, mix the sun-dried tomatoes, tuna, capers, plum tomatoes
and olives together. Season well.

Ingredients listed in green are available from Julian Graves

6. Pile the onion and parsley mixture on to the cooled pastry base and spread evenly, leaving a 1cm border around the edge. Top with the tomato and tuna mixture.

7. Beat the egg yolk with 1tbsp of cold water and brush the border with the glaze.

8. On a lightly floured surface, roll out the remaining pastry into a blanket, large enough to cover the mixture and the base. Put the blanket in place and gently press around the edges to form a seal. Mark this edge with a fork if desired before brushing the whole pie with egg glaze.

9. Return the pie to the oven for 15-20 minutes until the pastry is crisp and golden. Serve warm or cold.

chocolate brownies with chilli sauce

MAKES 9 SQUARES

115g butter, plus extra for greasing
170g caster sugar
2 eggs, beaten
1 tsp vanilla extract
55g plain flour
55g cocoa powder
1 tsp baking powder
2 tbsp milk

for the chocolate chilli sauce

juice of 1 orange
100g dark Continental chocolate, broken
3 tbsp golden syrup
dash of Zulu chilli sauce

to serve
icing sugar
lashings of whipped cream!

1. Preheat the oven to180C/350F/Gas Mark 4.

2. Grease an 18cm square cake tin and line with greaseproof paper. Lightly grease this with butter as well.

3. Using an electric whisk, cream together the butter and sugar until pale and fluffy. Gradually beat in the eggs and vanilla.

4. Sift the flour, cocoa powder and baking powder into the butter mixture and gently fold in the milk.

5. Spoon into the prepared tin and level out the top. Bake in the oven for 35-40 minutes. Allow to cool in the tin for 10 minutes. Remove from the tin and place on a cooling rack.

6. To make the chocolate chilli sauce, place the orange juice in a small pan, add the chocolate and stir over a low heat until melted. Stir in the golden syrup. Add a little dash of the Zulu sauce.

7. Cut the brownies into squares and dust with icing sugar. Serve with a generous drizzling of warm chocolate chilli sauce and cream.

syllabub trifle with spiced pears

SERVES 6

250g dried pears, halved
1 cinnamon stick
300ml sweet dessert wine
225g Madeira cake, sliced
250g raspberries
250g mascarpone cheese
300ml double cream
2 tbsp runny honey
finely grated zest and juice of 1 orange
50g dark chocolate, cut into shreds
small sprigs of mint
icing sugar to dust

1. Place the pears in a shallow pan with the cinnamon. Pour over the wine and 200ml water, cover and simmer for 25-30 minutes or until just tender, but keeping their shape. Remove the cinnamon stick and set aside to cool. (There should be about 150ml of liquid left with the pears.)

2. Arrange the Madeira cake in the base of a large glass serving dish. Drizzle over the cooled liquid from the pears. Scatter the pears and half the raspberries over the top. Set aside.

3. Place the mascarpone, cream, honey, orange zest and juice in a bowl and whisk until the mixture is smooth and forms soft peaks. Spoon this cream mixture evenly over the fruit layer. Chill.

4. Scatter over the remaining raspberries and chocolate. Decorate with mint sprigs and a good dusting of icing sugar before serving.

Ingredients listed in green are available from Julian Graves

apricot and marzipan shortcake

SERVES 6

140g butter, softened
50g caster sugar, plus extra for sprinkling
1 egg yolk
225g plain flour, plus extra for rolling
100g white marzipan, grated
2 x 411g cans apricots in fruit juice, drained well
1 egg, beaten
50g raw pistachio kernels, chopped

1. Beat together the butter and sugar until smooth. Mix in the egg yolk. With a flat-bladed knife, stir in the flour and bring together to form a soft dough. Wrap in clingfilm and chill for 1 hour.

2. Preheat the oven to 190C/375F/Gas Mark 5.

3. Roll out the dough on a lightly floured flat baking sheet to a 38cm round.

4. Scatter the marzipan over the pastry, leaving a 5cm border. Pile the apricots over the marzipan.

5. Roughly fold over the edges of pastry onto the apricots so they just overlap.

6. Brush with a little beaten egg and scatter over a little extra caster sugar.

7. Bake for 25-30 minutes or until golden and crisp. Sprinkle over the pistachios and serve warm with cream or custard.

espresso ice-cream cup

SERVES 2

4 scoops traditional vanilla ice-cream
300ml espresso coffee, freshly brewed
25g bitter Continental chocolate, grated
ground cinnamon for sprinkling
icing sugar for sprinkling
8 wafer biscuits

1. Spoon some ice-cream into two extra large coffee cups.

2. Pour over the freshly made espresso coffee to almost cover the ice-cream.

3. Top with a sprinkling of grated chocolate.

4. Finish with a light dusting of cinnamon and icing sugar and serve with wafer biscuits. Eat at once!

Lesley Waters

Cooks up a party

Exclusively written and prepared for

JULIAN GRAVES
LIMITED

INTRO

Hello I'm Lesley Waters and welcome to 'Cooking Up A Party' a collection of recipes guaranteed to make your party go with a swing. Cooking for a crowd doesn't have to be daunting and time consuming. To spend the maximum amount of time partying, simply mix and match a few dishes and in no time at all you'll have a feast for all your friends to enjoy.

For a no cook option Julian Graves has a fabulous selection of nuts, fruits, and savoury snacks to accompany dips and drinks or for a party feast get cooking these luxurious recipes and crack open the champagne.

Cheers!

Lesley

Lesley Waters

chocolate and fig baked tart

SERVES 8-10

350g ready-made shortcrust pastry
plain flour for rolling
150ml double cream
110g bitter Continental chocolate, broken into pieces
250g mascarpone cheese
2 eggs, beaten
250g soft juicy figs, roughly chopped

1. Preheat the oven to 190C/375F/Gas Mark 5.

2. On a lightly floured surface, roll out the pastry and use to line a 30cm loose-bottomed tart tin. Chill for 20 minutes.

3. Line the pastry case with greaseproof paper and fill with baking beans. Bake in the oven for 10-15 minutes. Remove the paper and beans and return to the oven for a further 3-5 minutes until just cooked. Remove from the oven and reduce the heat to 180C/375F/Gas Mark 4.

4. Place the cream and chocolate in a bowl over a pan of simmering water. Stir until the chocolate has just melted. Remove from the heat and add the mascarpone and beaten eggs. Stir in the figs.

5. Pour the chocolate and fig mixture into the cooked tart case and return to the oven for 20-25 minutes or until just set. (The top is supposed to crack!) Allow to cool.

6. Serve with crème fraîche or whipped cream.

Ingredients listed in green are available from Julian Graves

berry and hazelnut tart

SERVES 6

6 tbsp caster sugar
2 tsp ground cinnamon
350g ready-made shortcrust pastry
250g cream cheese
juice and finely grated rind of 1 large orange
2 tbsp icing sugar
250g mixed blueberries and raspberries
50g shelled hazelnuts, toasted and chopped
icing sugar for dusting

1. Preheat the oven to 200C/400F/Gas Mark 6. Line a baking sheet with baking parchment.

2. Mix together the caster sugar and cinnamon. On a dry surface, roll out the pastry in the sugar and cinnamon mixture until approximately 1cm thick.

3. Using a plate, cut out a neat round of about 23cm in diameter, and carefully place on to the lined baking tray. Prick the pastry all over with a fork and crimp the edges.

4. Bake the pastry in the oven for 10-12 minutes, or until cooked and biscuit coloured.

5. Allow the pastry to cool completely before carefully transferring to a serving plate.

6. In a small bowl beat the cream cheese with the orange juice and grated rind, adding the icing sugar to taste. Spread this mixture over the pastry base leaving a 2.5cm border clear. Top the orange cream with the berries and scatter over the hazelnuts. Lightly dust with icing sugar and serve straightaway.

exotic fruity tootie

SERVES 4

100g Lexia raisins
100g golden raisins
50g glacé cherries, quartered
60ml rum
75ml fresh orange juice
500ml tub of good-quality vanilla ice-cream
50g flaked almonds, toasted

1. Put the raisins and cherries into a bowl. Add the rum and orange juice and stir well. Set aside to soak for about 30 minutes.

2. Place the soaked fruit and any liquid into a small pan. Gently heat for 5 minutes.

3. Scoop the ice-cream into four serving dishes or glasses. Spoon over the fruity-tootie sauce and scatter over the almonds. Serve straightaway.

Ingredients listed in green are available from Julian Graves

HISTORY

Julian Graves started trading in 1987 when business partners and longtime friends Nick Shutts and Nigel Morris saw a niche in the marketplace and from humble beginnings, a single high street shop, built up a multi million pound operation.

In 1984, Nick, who had previously sold pre packed meat to the restaurant trade, borrowed £500 from his father to run a market stall in Moreton-in-Marsh selling traditional baking ingredients such as dried currants, raisins and sultanas. The products were sold straight from their cardboard boxes and were weighed and bagged on the stall.

The stall became so successful and demand so great that he decided to sell the produce already pre packed to increase the speed of sales. The range had also expanded to include cherries, walnuts and ground almonds,

Nick also began taking on stalls in other market locations and in newly created shopping malls, such as Merry Hill, in Dudley, and the Crowngate Shopping Centre, in Worcester.

By the time there were 12 such stalls, he realised it was time to invest in a high street shop, mainly to provide the necessary space for packaging and distributing the ever expanding stock range.

When that first shop opened in Brierley Hill High Street, in the West Midlands, in 1987, the business was originally called Food for Thought. But after Nigel Morris invested in the business in 1993, the two decided to use their middle names to create Julian (Nick's) Graves (Nigel's).

That year, the first Julian Graves shop opened in High Wycombe. In 1996, the company embarked on its first rapid expansion plan that led to a further 85 shops and retail outlets opening by 2001.

In 2000, the business moved into new 21,000 sq ft premises, comprising a head office, warehouse and processing facility, at the Pensnett Industrial Estate, Kingswinford.

A year later, it received the prestigious 'Rising Star of the Year' award from Retail Week and a further nomination from The Birmingham Post for Midlands Entrepreneur of the Year, sponsored by Ernst & Young.

The company is currently partway through its second ambitious expansion phase, and has now grown to around 200 outlets.

Not bad going for a business that started as a market stall in the Cotswolds.

For more information about Julian Graves visit our website **www.juliangraves.co.uk**

Disclaimer

Should you have any comments or queries about any of these recipes please let us know via email – snacks@juliangraves.co.uk. Please note that oven temperatures do vary on individual manufacturers' appliances and we would recommend that you refer to the manufacturers' handbook.

JULIAN GRAVES
— LIMITED —

£2.99

www.juliangraves.co.uk